FOREWORD

For the past three and a half years, H
undertaken the painstaking research   her
splendid book *Lost Lives*. The end r   men
of Countesthorpe and the surrounding villages of Kilby, Peatling ~~gna,~~
Peatling Parva and Shearsby who made the supreme sacrifice for their
King and Country during the First and Second World Wars.
The author's travels took her to the National Archives at Kew, the Record
Office for Leicestershire, Leicester and Rutland and to many surviving
families locally.
Contact with descendants, both locally and nationally, has been time
consuming but rewarding. The names of two men, who lost their lives
in the First World War, had not been included on the Countesthorpe War
Memorial, this omission is now to be rectified.
Henrietta has made an enormous contribution to the social and military
history of her community for which she is owed a huge debt of gratitude.

August 2007   Derek Seaton
                                           Historian and Author

Contents

Foreword

World War I

Countesthorpe
Reuben Boat 2
Donald Neville Cadoux 2
John Alfred Chapman 4
John Sydney Coleman 5
Busby Cox 6
Joseph William Cox 6
Stephen Leonard Elliott 7
Herman Edward Findley 8
Reuben Flude Gamble 9
William Armston Gamble 10
Thomas Garrett 11
Joseph Horace Gilliam 12
Sydney Gillam 13
George Adolphus Glass 14
Norman Cyril John Harrison 15
Dennis Heathcote 16
Walter Edwin Herbert 17
William Job Arthur Herbert 18
Wilfred Herbert 19
John Hubbard 19
Joseph Henry Hubbard 20
Wilfred Henry Hubbard 21
Cecil Frederick Immins 21
Edwin Immins 22
Henry William Emmanuel Jarratt 23
Alfred Arthur Johnson 24
William Johnson 25
John Thomas Lord 26
William Herbert Lord 27
Ernest Mason 27
Alfred Oldershaw 28
Harry Oldershaw 28
Ernest Richard Olive 29
Walter Charles Peet 30
William Simms 31

John Cawrey Soars 32
Alfred William Stafford 33
Herbert Swann 34
Fred Thornton 35
Joseph Henry Tilley 36
Frank Veasey 36
Harry Veasey 37
Hurbert Veasey 37
Edwin Charles Wallis 37
Horace Samuel Wallis 39
Arthur Wells 40
Sydney Weston 41
Albert Ernest Yorke 42
Frederick York 42

Kilby
Thomas Haines 44
Charles Hassell 44
John Abbott Pask 45
Frank Wormleighton 45

Peatling Magna
White Chesterson 48
Henry Cook(e) 48
Allen Marshall 49
Edward James Tilley 50
William Edward Tilley 51

Peatling Parva
Thomas Glenn 54
Thomas Lee 54
W. Phillips 54
Herbert Prentice 55
Jasper Charles Stewart 56
George Alfred Tarratt 57
William Woodward 58

Shearsby
Lionel Sidney Burton 60
William Clowes 61
Horace Alfred Hensman 62
Robert Simons 63
J.S. Watts 63

Contents

World War II

Countesthorpe
John Patrick Barrett..........................66
Robert Sidney Brothwell..................67
Douglas Arthur Chapman 68
John Keith Chapman.......................69
Henry Ernest Creasey 70
Leslie Ernest Cutler.........................71
Thomas Leonard Fielding...............72
Victor Clarence Fretter....................73
Thomas Charles Hill 74
Gwilym Rhys Hughes.....................75
Larrad Lionel T.J. Lucas 76
Ronald Henry Mason......................77
Dennis Frederic Moore 78
Leonard Norton...............................79
John Parsons...................................80
Harry Riddington 81
Norman Alfred Smith.....................82
Thomas Frank Spiby......................83

Peatling Parva
Phillip Hunt.....................................86
Cameron Lawrie..............................86
Sidney George Turner.....................87

Shearsby
Maurice Arthur Garner....................90

Short History of the
Leicestershire Regiment..................91

Acknowledgments...........................94

THE GREAT WAR
COUNTESTHORPE'S WAR DEAD

Reuben Boat

Rank: Private
Number: 25850
Decorations:
Regiment, Corps etc:
9th Battalion, Leicestershire Regiment
Military Service: Boat attested for military service at the age of 30 years on 6 December 1915. After basic training with the 3rd Leicesters, he sailed from Folkestone on 10 August 1916 to join the 9th Battalion on 29 August 1916.
Date and circumstances of Death: Boat was killed in action, during the attack on the village of Gueudecourt, part of the battle of Morval, on 25 September 1916.
Age: 30
Buried: Boat has no known grave. He is commemorated on the Thiepval Memorial (Pier and Face 2, C and 3A)
Family: Boat was the only son of Louisa Boat, who later married Henry Baker. The family lived in Central Street, Countesthorpe. Reuben was employed in the hosiery trade before his enlistment. He was unmarried.

Donald Neville Cadoux

Number: 201
Regiment, Corps etc:
3rd Field Ambulance, Australian Medical Corps
Military Service: Cadoux had served for three years in the 1st (Volunteer) Battalion of the Leicestershire Regiment and for one year with the 2nd (Volunteer) Battalion) of the Gloucestershire Regiment. He enlisted with the Australian Imperial Force on 21 August 1914. He was posted to the 3rd Field Ambulance (Australian Army Medical Corps) and embarked aboard the transport *Medic* at Fremantle on 2 November 1914 for the Middle East and Gallipoli.
Date and circumstances of Death: Cadoux was killed in action on 25 April 1915, as the boat carrying his section ("C") of the Field Ambulance neared the shore at Gallipoli. The boat came under heavy Turkish fire, suffering at least five casualties. Cadoux was, according to the testimony of his comrades, killed instantly by a shot to the heart. He seems to have been carried in the boat back to the transports; thereby causing some confusion as to the date of his death, which is sometimes given as 3 May 1915. The War diary of his

unit records Cadoux as "missing, probably drowned" and "since reported dead", which probably can be attributed to the confusion of the landings and the early disappearance of his body.
Age: 30
Buried: Donald Cadoux is commemorated on the Lone Pine Memorial, Gallipoli. His name has not yet been added to the Countesthorpe memorial.
Family: Donald Cadoux was born at Countesthorpe on 27 June 1884, the son of Charles and Susan Cadoux. His father, Charles Cadoux was a Spinners' Agent. Their home was at Colbrook House, Cosby Road, Countesthorpe.
Notes: Donald was educated first at the Wyggeston Boys' School, Leicester and then trained as an engineer, serving a five year apprenticeship with Barron & Co. of Leicester. He emigrated to Western Australia in about 1909, working as an engineer in Perth, before moving to the Wongan Hills area in 1913. He intended to farm and established a settlement that was subsequently (in 1928) named Cadoux in his honour.

He is reputed to have dug a 100 foot well to find water. A tablet to his memory was destroyed in an earthquake in 1959, though his medals and bronze commemorative plaque are proudly displayed in its place.

Countesthorpe War Memorial November 1921.

John Alfred Chapman

John Alfred Chapman with Wife Sarah & son Douglas Arthur

Rank: Able Seaman
Number: R/4877
Decorations: War medals
Regiment, Corps etc:
Hood Battalion, 63rd (Royal Naval) Division
Military Service:
Date and circumstances of Death:
Killed in action on 16 February 1918 on Welsh Ridge, near Marcoing, during the battle of the Ancre.
Age: 30. He was born on 18 September 1887.

Buried: According to his memorial in St Andrew's church, Countesthorpe, Chapman was first buried NE of Villers-Plouich and SSW of Cambrai. He was later reburied at the Fifteen Ravine British Cemetery at Villers-Plouich (grave VII.D.2). He is also mentioned on his widow's headstone in Countesthorpe Cemetery.

Family: Chapman was the second child and eldest son of Henry Chapman and Emily Jarratt. He had five sisters and three brothers. All the brothers were employed in the building trade, in which his father had a small business. He married Sarah Cox at the parish church, Countesthorpe, on 12 September 1912. His son was born in 1917. His widow died, without remarrying, on 8 June 1970.

Notes: Chapman was educated at the village school and sang, with his father, brothers and sisters, in the church choir.

John Sydney Coleman

Rank: Sergeant
Number: 11520
Regiment, Corps etc:
'D' Company, 8th Battalion, Leicestershire Regiment
Military Service:
Date and circumstances of Death:
3 a.m. on 24 September 1915. It is likely that Sergeant Coleman was the one man recorded as killed that day in his battalion's War Diary. He had, apparently, gone with a party to examine and complete cuts in the barbed wire in front of the British trenches – ordered by the Brigadier, who was keen that any advance should not be hindered by 'friendly' fire.
Age: 22
Buried: Berles-au-Bois churchyard extension (S.13)

Family: Coleman was born on 4 January 1893 in Burnley, Lancashire. He was the youngest of the five children of Harry Coleman and his wife, Elizabeth (Rawlinson). Harry Coleman moved to Countesthorpe on his appointment as headmaster of the school in Main Street. The family home was Ivydene, in Station Road. John Coleman's brother, Cecil Rawlins Coleman prospered as a businessman in Leicester. He acquired Launde Abbey, which he later presented to the Leicester Diocese.
John Coleman did not marry.

IVYDENE, Home on Station Road of John Sidney Coleman (WWI) and Thomas Leonard Fielding (WWII)

BUSBY COX
Rank: Private
Number: 20516
Regiment, Corps etc:
9th Battalion,
Leicestershire Regiment
Date and circumstances of Death:
Killed in action on 14 July 1916.
Busby Cox was one of several Countesthorpe men killed in the attack on Bazentin-le-Petit Wood on 14 and 15 July 1916. Skirting Mametz Wood on the way to their objective, Cox's battalion came under heavy machine gun and artillery fire from hitherto undetected German positions. There were heavy casualties there and on the edge of Bazentin Wood itself, which was never fully cleared of the enemy.
Age: 23
Buried: His name appears on the memorial at Thiepval (Pier and face 2c and 3a)
Family: Busby Cox was the son of Betsy Wilson (formerly Gilliam) of Peatling End, Countesthorpe. He was born on 8 January 1893. His birth certificate shows his name as Busby Cox Wilson. The certificate does not record the name of his father. Betsy married Henry Cox, a framework knitter of Countesthorpe, in 1917.

JOSEPH WILLIAM COX
Rank: Private
Number: 201716
Regiment, Corps etc:
1/4th Battalion,
Leicestershire Regiment
Date and circumstances of Death:
Died of wounds, 29 April 1918
Age: 23
Buried: Pernes British Cemetery, Grave 11.A.9
Family: Joseph William Cox was the brother of Busby Cox.

Foston Road Cemetery, Countesthorpe

STEPHEN LEONARD ELLIOTT

Rank: Sergeant
Number: 19315
Regiment, Corps etc:
6th Battalion, Royal Field Artillery
Date and circumstances of Death:
23 June 1917
Age: 41
Buried: Sergeant Elliott's name is recorded on the Kirkee 1914-1918 Memorial, India. His name has not yet been added to the Countesthorpe memorial.

Family: Stephen was the son of Thomas Elliott and his wife, Sarah Ann Cox (who were married at Countesthorpe on 2 October 1871). He was one of seven children; having four brothers (Albert, Joyce, Taylor and Oscar) and two sisters (Sarah and Rose).
Notes: Stephen Elliott was employed before his enlistment as a wagon repairer.

Inspection of Countesthorpe ex-servicemen by The Duke of York before the unveiling of the War Memorial. November 1921

HERMAN EDWARD FINDLEY

Rank: Private
Number: 25809
Regiment, Corps etc:
6th Battalion,
Leicestershire Regiment
Date and circumstances of Death:
Killed in action on 24 March 1917. From 17th to 27th March Findley's battalion occupied trenches in the Hohenzollern sector of the front line, near Vermelles.
Age: 27
Buried: Vermelles British Cemetery, Plot 5, Row A, Grave 39.
Family: Herman Findley was born at Countesthorpe on 25 April 1890. He was the youngest child of Thomas Findley (a framework knitter) and his wife, Elizabeth Heathcote. Herman was one of five boys and had five sisters. He attended Countesthorpe National School on Main Street. He was unmarried.
Notes: Herman probably worked in the hosiery trade. He sang in the church choir.

Herman Edward Findley

REUBEN FLUDE GAMBLE

Rank: Private
Number: 18249
Regiment, Corps etc:
9th Battalion,
Leicestershire Regiment
Military Service:
Date and circumstances of Death:
like Busby Cox, Reuben Gamble was killed in action on 14th July 1916 as their battalion took part in the attack on Bazentin-le-Petit Wood.
Age: 29
Buried: His name appears on the memorial at Thiepval
Family: Reuben was the brother of William Armston Gamble
Notes: In 1901 (aged 12) he was recorded on the census as working as a hosiery winder.

Pte. REUBEN GAMBLE, Leicester Regt., killed in action on July 14. His parents live at 43, Albion-road, Sileby.

Leicester Mercury

WILLIAM ARMSTON GAMBLE

Rank: Corporal
Number: 2266
Decorations: Military Medal
Regiment, Corps etc:
4th Battalion, Leicestershire Regiment
Military Service: William Gamble enlisted in the 4th Battalion, Leicestershire Regiment, at Leicester, on 10 August 1914 (less than a week after Britain's declaration of war). Having undergone his basic training at Luton, Gamble was posted to the British Expeditionary Force in France and Flanders, where he served with the 1/4th Battalion of the Leicesters from 2 March 1915 until 7 December 1916. In February 1915 he was promoted to the rank of lance corporal. On 13 October 1915 Gamble was just one of over 450 casualties suffered by his battalion in the disastrous assault on the Hohenzollern Redoubt. He was fortunate enough to be carried back from the front by ambulance to Casualty Clearing Station No. 9 and thence to No. 16 General Hospital at Le Treport. From there he was discharged, on 15 November 1915, to the Base at Rouen. On 24 November 1915 he rejoined his unit. In January 1916 the battalion was withdrawn from the frontline and spent a restful three weeks awaiting transport to Egypt. At the last minute however, Gamble's battalion was disembarked from the troopships and carried across France to the frontline opposite Vimy Ridge. From there they moved to the Somme. In July 1916 Gamble received his second corporal's stripe.
Notes: Gamble's enlistment papers give his occupation as 'hosiery hand'.

Thomas Garrett

Rank: Private
Number: 292818
Regiment, Corps etc: 15th Battalion, Cheshire Regiment
Date and circumstances of Death: 27th March 1918
Age: 18
Buried: Recorded on the Pozieres Memorial, panels 35-36.
Family: Thomas was the son of William and Elizabeth Garrett. William Garrett was born in Narborough and his wife came from Stoke on Trent. They settled in Countesthorpe in about 1890. One of Thomas's brothers, Charles Nehemiah, also served in the Great War. He had three sisters and another brother, as well as a half sister and brother. He was unmarried.

Unveiling of the War Memorial by The Duke of York. November 1921   Photo: P.H. Adams

- 11 -

JOSEPH HORACE GILLIAM

Rank: Private
Number: 27157
Regiment, Corps etc:
1st Battalion the Leicestershire Regiment
Military Service: Gilliam attested in Leicester on 11 December 1915. He was posted first to the 12th Battalion and then, at the end of August 1916, to the Leicester's 1st Battalion. The battalion was heavily engaged at the end of August and through September 1916 on the Somme. During a lull, on 19 October, when the battalion was employed in carrying supplies up to the front, Gilliam was reported 'missing'. He rejoined the battalion on 9 November 1916 but was absent again from the last day of 1916 until 28 April 1917, possibly in hospital. In September 1917 Gilliam was with his battalion, occupying part of the line between Loos and St Elie.
Date and circumstances of Death: On 12 September 1917 the battalion's war diary records "Boche very active with artillery immediately on our right". Gilliam died of wounds the following day, when the diary noted "quiet day in the line".
Age: 29 years and 9 months in December 1915

Buried: Bethune Town Cemetery, VI.G.48
Family: Gilliam was unmarried. He was the son of Joseph and Rebecca Gilliam of Church Street, Countesthorpe. The father was recorded in the 1901 census as partially paralysed. Joseph Horace had two older siblings: Lucy and Herbert Thomas, both of whom were living in Church Street at the time of enlistment.
Notes: Joseph Horace was employed in the hosiery trade. In March 1918, as his next of kin, Gilliam's mother received back his personal effects from the Officer in charge of Infantry Records at Lichfield. They included his identity disc, letters, photographs, cards, pipe, a religious book, purse, razor, steel mirror, snuff box, badge and canvas photograph case.

Joseph Horace Gilliam mentioned on his parents grave stone in Foston Road cemetery, Countesthorpe

SYDNEY GILLAM

Rank: Private
Number: 21587
Regiment, Corps etc:
6th Battalion, Leicestershire Regiment
Military Service:
Date and circumstances of Death:
Gillam died in the Leicester Royal Infirmary, of a diabetic coma, on 26 January 1919.
Age: 28 (The 1891 census records Gillam as 10 months old)
Buried: He was buried in the same grave as his father (number 153) in the Foston Road Cemetery, Countesthorpe.
Family: Sydney Gillam was the only son of Henry Gillam and his wife, Mary Elizabeth Veasey. He had three sisters; Eveline, Doris Kathleen, and Nellie. Only Nellie lived long enough to marry and have children.
Notes: Sydney Gillam's death is not recorded by the Commonwealth war Graves Commission

Sidney Gillam pictured with his stepfather, William Henry Cox

George Adolphus Glass
Rank: Private
Number: 27157
Regiment, Corps etc:
9th Battalion, Sherwood Foresters (Notts & Derbys Regiment)
Military Service: Although his attestation and service papers do not survive at the National Archives, his pay book is still extant and tells us that Glass enlisted on 18 October 1915. He was posted to France on 4 September 1916.
Date and circumstances of Death: Glass was killed in action on 4th October 1917, at the close of the fighting for Polygon Wood; part of the offensive in Flanders in the Autumn of 1917.
Age: 20 (approximately)
Buried: Glass's burial place is unknown. He is commemorated on panels 99-102 and 162-162A of the Tyne Cot Memorial.
Family: George Glass was born (in about 1898) in Leicester Road, Countesthorpe; the eldest child of Henry Alphonsus Glass, a carpenter from Portsmouth and Emma Burley, a native of Countesthorpe.

Private George Adolphus Glass

NORMAN CYRIL JOHN HARRISON

Rank: Private
Number: 41591
Regiment, Corps etc: 'A' Company, 18th Battalion The Manchester Regiment
Military Service: Harrison enlisted at Leicester on 15 November 1915. He was sent then to the 21st Reserve Battalion, Lancashire Fusiliers and afterwards through the 72nd Training Reserve Battalion to the East Lancashire Regiment. On 28 October 1916, whilst in France, he was transferred again, to the 18th Manchesters. Photographs show him in uniform, booted and spurred, so it seems likely that, given his ability with horses, Harrison was employed with the battalion transport.
Date and circumstances of Death: Died of wounds (possibly gas) 13 June 1917, during the 3rd Battle of Ypres.
Age: 20
Buried: Hop Store Cemetery, Vlamertinghe, Belgium: Plot I, Row B, Grave 43.
Family: Norman Harrison was brought up at the Countesthorpe Cottage Homes, where his father was Superintendent and his mother, Matron.
Notes: Harrison's enlistment papers give his occupation as a farm labourer. He came from farming stock in Cumberland, where his three (paternal) uncles all had farms. Harrison, according to family tradition, was a competent amateur artist and violinist.

Private Harrison pictured with his family

DENNIS HEATHCOTE

Rank: Private
Number: 40479
Regiment, Corps etc:
18th Battalion, Prince of Wales Own (West Yorkshire) Regiment.
Date and circumstances of Death:
10 May 1917
Age: 27
Buried: He is recorded on the Arras Memorial (Bay 4).
Family: Dennis was the eldest of four sons of Robert and Bertha Ann Heathcote (née Boat). He and his brothers (Herbert, Joseph and Ernest) were brought up at the bottom of Green Lane, Countesthorpe, where their mother kept a small shop. Robert Heathcote died in May 1900. Bertha lived until her 87th year, dying in 1957.

Private Dennis Heathcote

Walter Edwin Herbert

Rank: Private
Number: 202064
Regiment, Corps etc:
9th Battalion Sherwood Foresters (Nottinghamshires & Derbyshire Regiment).
Military Service: Herbert enlisted on the 9 December 1915, giving his age as 22 years and 11 months. He was trained as a Lewis Gunner. In May 1917 Herbert suffered a brief period of sickness, returning to duty on 16 June 1917 in time for the 3rd Battle of Ypres (better known as Paschendaele). He was wounded in action on 6 September 1917 but fit again by 21 September. On 14 October he was wounded again in the legs and arms. This proved to be a 'Blighty' wound and he was taken back to England aboard the *Grantully Castle*, a 552 bed hospital ship, on 28 October 1917. Herbert was well enough to return home on furlough from 16 March to 28 March 1918 and to return to France on 13 June 1918
Date and circumstances of Death: Herbert was killed in action on 3 October 1918, during the advance on Cambrai.

Age: 25
Buried: Haynecourt British Cemetery, Nord, France. Plot II, B3.
Family: Walter Edwin was the son of Edwin and Matilda Herbert (nee Hall). He had three brothers and three sisters. Walter Edwin was unmarried at the time of his death. He had been employed as a hosiery trimmer, dyeing and finishing. Like his parents he was a member of the Baptist Church.

WILLIAM JOB ARTHUR HERBERT

Rank: Sergeant
Number: L/4003
Regiment, Corps etc:
5th Irish Lancers
Military Service: Attested Glen Parva Depot. Transfered to 5th Irish Lancers and served in Ireland. At the time of his death he was serving with the Kings African Rifles.
Date and circumstances of Death: Herbert was killed in Portugese East Africa now Malawi.
Age: 22
Buried: Mongochi, Malawi
Family: He was the son of Job Herbert 1833-1923 and Dorothy Snodin 1866-1968. Herbert had one sister and three brothers.

Private William Job Arthur Herbert

WILFRED HERBERT
Rank: Private
Number: 25227
Regiment, Corps etc:
8th Battalion, Leicestershire Regiment
Date and circumstances of Death:
Wilfred Herbert was another local man to fall in the attack on Bazentin Wood on 15 July 1916. Having failed to reach their final objective, Herbert's battalion dug in on the edge of Bazentin Wood and village and attempted to beat off the German counter-attacks. They were relieved on 16 July, having suffered over 500 casualties.
Age: 19
Buried: Commemorated on the Thiepval memorial
Family: Wilfred was the youngest of the seven children of Walter Herbert, a framework-knitter, and his wife Sarah Ann. Wilfred is recorded on the 1901 census, aged 4 years, living with his family at Station Road, Countesthorpe.

JOHN HUBBARD
Rank: Private
Number: 25155
Regiment, Corps etc:
2nd and 4th Battalions, Leicestershire Regiment
Date and circumstances of Death:
24 March 1918
Age: 27
Buried: Commemorated on the Arras Memorial, Bay 5
Family: John was the son of William Henry Hubbard and his wife, Emma Morris; both natives of Countesthorpe. William Henry Hubbard was a butcher, with his home and shop in Main Street, Countesthorpe. On 18 March 1916, John Hubbard married Annie Harrison, the daughter of George William Harrison, at St Peter's church, Whetstone. John was already serving in the army. John's widow later remarried and moved to the Northampton area. There were no children of the first marriage.

JOSEPH HENRY HUBBARD

Rank: Private
Number: 9278
Regiment, Corps etc: 1st Battalion The Warwickshire Regiment
Military Service: It is likely that Hubbard was a regular soldier, or reservist, and so sailed with the BEF to France in August 1914. He was captured, perhaps wounded, at some time during the retreat from Mons and died in German hands, on 24 September 1914.
Age: 35
Buried: The Niederzwehren Cemetery, Kassel, Hessen, Germany. Grave IV.B. 4. The cemetery was begun in 1915 and was expanded after the War as smaller cemeteries were amalgamated. It is unclear where Hubbard was originally buried.
Family: Joseph was one of three sons (and five daughters) of Charles Hubbard and Mary Herbert. The family lived in Green Lane, Counntesthorpe. Charles Hubbard worked as a general labourer. Joseph had been a hosiery knitter but at the time of his marriage, on 13 July 1910, to Louisa Bandy, the daughter of Charles Bandy, he gave his occupation as railway platelayer. Joseph and Louisa had two sons. The first, George Alvin, born on 12 October 1912, died at the age of 6 on 15 October 1919. The second, Joseph Eric, was born on 5 November 1915 and lived until 17 December 2002. He married Doris May Williams at the Methodist Church in Countesthorpe, on 25 May 1935.

Notes: The Leicester Chronicle of 26 November 1921 included a photograph of Louisa Hubbard and her son, Joseph Eric, at the unveiling of the war memorial. Louisa's husband was the first Countesthorpe man to be killed in the Great War.

Leicester Chronicle Photograph

WILFRED HENRY HUBBARD

Rank: Private
Number: 11359
Regiment, Corps etc:
2nd Battalion, Leicestershire Regiment
Military Service: Wilfred Hubbard attested for six years' service with the Special Reserve (the old militia) on 5 May 1914. His attestation papers show that he was under age (17 years and 147 days) and under size (5 feet and 2³/₈ inches tall). He was posted to the 2nd Battalion, Leicestershire Regiment; embarking at Southampton on 10 November 1915 to join the battalion in France. After less than a month on the Western Front however, Hubbard, with the rest of his battalion, was taken by train to Marseilles and thence by the transport, *Royal George*, to Basra. He arrived at Basra on the last day of 1915. The 2nd Leicesters were part of the advance in Mesopotamia against the Turks. The climate and its associated problems of unclean water and disease, took a heavy toll of the British and Indian forces. Hubbard himself was committed to hospital three times; spending over eight weeks in hospital between 11 January and 14 May 1916. On 15 July 1916 he was found asleep at his post – a most serious offence on active service – and committed for trial by court martial. On 17 July 1916 he was tried and found guilty. His sentence was to suffer death by being shot but this was commuted to two years' imprisonment with hard labour. After another brief spell in hospital, Hubbard was returned to active service, his sentence having been suspended.
Date and circumstances of Death:
On 27 October 1916 Hubbard was seriously wounded, with a gunshot wound to the head. He died the next day.
Age: 19
Buried: Amara War Cemetery, Iraq
Family: Wilfred was the son of Thomas Henry Hubbard and his wife, Emma Orton. Thomas was from Wigston Magna and his wife from Blaby. In 1919 the family, including five brothers and four sisters, was resident in Church Street, Countesthorpe.
Notes: At the time of his attestation, Wilfred was employed as a farm labourer.

Cecil Frederick Immins

Rank: Private
Number: 13867
Regiment, Corps etc:
1st Battalion,
King's Own Scottish Borderers
Military Service: Immins' battalion landed at Cape Helles on the Gallipoli Peninsula on 25 April 1915. He was killed in one of the attempts to drive back the Turkish defenders, who occupied high ground, dominating the landing beaches and preventing an advance inland.
Date and circumstances of Death: Immins was killed at the start of the 3rd Battle of Krithia, the preliminary attacks on Turkish trenches in the Helles area of Gallipoli, intended ultimately to capture the heights of Achi Baba.
Age: 19
Buried: Commemorated on the Helles Memorial, at the tip of the Gallipoli Peninsula, Turkey.
Family: Cecil Frederick was the second of three sons of John Thomas Immins, a framework-knitter, and Mary Jane Miles. The family moved from Cox's Lane, Central Street, Countesthorpe, to 20, Bushloe End, Wigston Magna. Cecil Frederick was unmarried.

Edwin Immins

Rank: Private
Number: 61422
Regiment, Corps etc:
12th (Duke of Lancaster's Own Yeomanry) Battalion, The Manchester Regiment.
Military Service:
Date and circumstances of Death:
Age: c. 37
Buried: Grave IV.L.5 at the A.I.F. Burial Ground, Flers, department of the Somme.
Family: Edwin was the youngest son of John Immins and Mary Keen. He was born at Countesthorpe.

HENRY WILLIAM EMMANUEL JARRATT

Rank: Lance sergeant
Number: 7011
Regiment, Corps etc:
No. 3 Company, 2nd Battalion, Coldstream Guards
Military Service: Jarratt attested for military service at Leicester on 7 November 1906. He gave his age as 19 years and 5 months. He was 5 feet 7^1/$_8$ inches tall and weighed 132½ pounds. Jarratt had seen some service already with the 3rd Battalion, Leicestershire Regiment (the old militia) but now opted for the Coldstream Guards. After six months' service (and a gymnastics course) his height had increased to 5 feet and 7 ¼ inches and he weighed 12½ pounds more. Army life seems to have suited Jarratt. He gained his third and second class certificates of education and passed classes of instruction in signalling and swimming. In 1908 he extended his period of service, to complete seven years with the colours, rather than on the reserve. In February 1911, he was promoted to lance corporal. In 1913 he transferred to the reserve but within a year, on 5 August 1914 (the day after war was declared) he was mobilised again and posted to the 2nd Battalion. Within a week he had been promoted to corporal and sent overseas with the British Expeditionary force.

Date and circumstances of Death: Jarratt was killed in action at Cuinchy, on 4 February 1915.
Age: 27
Buried: Cuinchy Cemetery, section F, number 9. He is also recorded on his parents' gravestone in Countesthorpe Cemetery.
Family: Henry was the son of Isaac Jarratt and his wife, Mary Starmer, of Cosby. He had four sisters: Annie Rebecca, Diana, Eveline and Elizabeth Mary. All were resident at Peatling Road, Countesthorpe in 1919.

Family gravestone, Countesthorpe

ALFRED ARTHUR JOHNSON

Rank: Private
Number: 77419
Regiment, Corps etc:
22nd Battalion,
Durham Light Infantry
Military Service:
Date and circumstances of Death:
26th March 1918
Age: about 19
Buried: Pargny British cemetery,
Somme, France IV.D. 10
Family: Youngest child of William
Payne Johnson and Sarah Jarratt.
Alfred had three sisters and a
brother, William, who was also in
the Durham Light Infantry.
Notes: He was unmarried

Alfred Arthur Johnson photographed as a young boy at home

WILLIAM JOHNSON
Rank: Private
Number: 1683
Regiment, Corps etc:
54th Battalion
Australian Imperial Force
Military Service: Johnson enlisted in Dubbo, New South Wales on 6 November 1915, at the age of 27 years and 9 months. On 14 April 1916 he sailed aboard the *Ceramic*, with reinforcements for the newly formed 54th Battalion, AIF, arriving at Suez on 17 May 1916. From Egypt the battalion moved to France. Johnson suffered several bouts of illness, including mild attacks of influenza and measles. On 7 January 1918 he was attached for duty to the Australian Army Ordnance Corps, returning to the 54th Battalion on 17 May.
Date and circumstances of Death: Killed in action near Amiens on 11 July 1918.
Age: 30
Buried: The Franvillers Communal Cemetery Extension (II.A.1).
Family: William was the son of Robert and Hannah Johnson. He was born in Wilby, Suffolk and resident in New South Wales. His widowed mother was living in Countesthorpe at the time of his death.

Private William Johnson

JOHN THOMAS LORD

Rank: Private
Number: 15617
Regiment, Corps etc:
6th Battalion, Leicestershire Regiment
Military Service: John Lord attested for military service at Leicester on 9 October 1914. He was posted to the Regimental Depot on 12 October 1914 and from there to the 6th Battalion, Leicestershire Regiment on 25 October. Following basic training and instruction as a signaller, Lord and his battalion were transferred to France, landing at Le Havre on 29 July 1915. Lord recorded in his diary that he first saw action in the trenches near Kemmel on Friday, 13 August 1915. Thereafter he records work as a signaller, in and out of the front-line, and periods of rest, parades and washing. He often wrote home to his wife and family. On 17 November 1915 he recorded "Go sick at Berle-Au-Bois" from where he was passed to a casualty clearing station and then back to England. He arrived at Boscombe a week later and records a gradual recovery, being allowed out of bed by 20 December and on 28 December venturing out of the hospital for the first time, to attend a concert. The diary entries cease that day.

John Thomas Lord & family. This picture was produced about three years after his death

Date and circumstances of Death: Lord died at the Hospital for Sick and Wounded at Boscombe, Hampshire, on 17 January 1916. The cause was given as cardiac failure and inflammation of the tonsils, due to field operations.
Age: 38
Buried: Foston Road Cemetery, Countesthorpe (grave number 24).
Family: John Thomas Lord was one of the six children of John Lord (a framework-knitter) and his wife, Ann Herbert. He married Patience Mary Asher, the daughter of Daniel Asher (a framework-knitter) on 2 April 1902, at the Countesthorpe Primitive Methodist Church.
Notes: At his attestation Lord gave his occupation as "Railway worker".

WILLIAM HERBERT LORD
Rank: Private
Number: 23044
Regiment, Corps etc:
11th Battalion,
Leicestershire Regiment
Military Service: William Lord's battalion was also known as the 'Midland Pioneers', wearing a pick and shovel badge as well as the Leicestershire Regiment's tiger. In October 1916 they were near Guillemont, on the Somme, providing working parties to make and repair trenches and trackways. Others served as stretcher bearers. On 15 October private Lord was in one of two companies employed in trench digging across newly captured ground. They came under enemy bombardment and Lord and one of his comrades were killed, their corporal and another wounded.
Date and circumstances of Death: 15 October 1916
Age: 20
Buried: Thiepval Memorial
Family: William Lord was born at Rugby, on 2 July 1896. He was the son of William Lord and his wife, Anna Swann. William was the nephew of John Thomas Lord.

ERNEST MASON
Rank: Lance-corporal
Number: 11516
Regiment, Corps etc:
8th Battalion,
Leicestershire Regiment
Date and circumstances of Death: Ernest Mason was yet another Countesthorpe man to fall at Bazentin Wood on 15 July 1916. His battalion had attacked the day before and held grimly onto a corner of the wood and Bazentin village until relieved the next day. Mason was one of sixty-six men of the 8th Leicesters killed.
Age: c. 31
Buried: His name is recorded on the Thiepval Memorial
Family: Ernest was the son of Alfred and Mary Jane Mason, of Wigston Magna. He married Rose Elliott, of Countesthorpe, at St Andrew's church, on 3 August 1908. They had one child, a son, named Arthur.
Notes: Ernest was employed as a house painter.

Ernest Mason & Rose Elliott's wedding 3rd August 1908. St Andrew's Church

Alfred Oldershaw

Rank: Lance-corporal
Number: 25588
Regiment, Corps etc:
55th Company, Royal Engineers
Military Service: Oldershaw's company was attached first to the 7th Division, serving with the BEF. He transferred with it to the Guards Division in September 1915.
Date and circumstances of Death: Died 28 October 1915
Age: 22
Buried: Longuenesse Souvenir Cemetery, St Omer; grave reference III.A.7.
Family: Alfred was one of the six sons and five daughters of Alfred Oldershaw and his wife, Lillie (Hartnell). He was born on 24th December 1892.

Harry Oldershaw

Rank: Private
Number: 4004
Regiment, Corps etc:
5th (Royal Irish) Lancers
Military Service: Harry Oldershaw was a regular soldier, having enlisted at the age of 16 with his friend William Herbert (who was numbered 4003). His regiment was serving with the 2nd Cavalry Division of the British Expeditionary Force. He died, presumably, at the casualty clearing station near the cemetery where he was buried.
Date and circumstances of Death: Died 22nd February 1915
Age: 19
Buried: Hazebrouck Communal Cemetery, grave reference III.A.35.
Family: Harry was the son of Alfred and Lillie Oldershaw and brother of the Alfred who is also recorded here.
Notes: He was unmarried.

ERNEST RICHARD OLIVE

Rank: Corporal
Number: 419300
Regiment, Corps etc:
2/2nd (North Midland) Field Ambulance, Royal Army Medical Corps
Military Service: The 2/2nd Field Ambulance was attached to the 59th (North Midland) Division. After service in Ireland, at the time of the Easter Rising in 1916, the division was transferred to the Western Front.
Date and circumstances of Death: A letter from his friend, Private L Riley, to Mrs Olive records that Corporal Olive was killed instantly by shrapnel on the morning of 27th September 1917.
Age: 21
Buried: Although he was originally buried near St Jean, North of Ypres, in 1921 his, like a number of other burials, was relocated to the New Irish Farm Cemetery, St Jean, Ypres (Ieper) Belgium (Row 'D' grave 3).

Corporal Ernist Richard Olive

Family: Ernest was the son of William Olive and his wife, Eliza Snutch. He had two sisters and a brother who served in the Leicestershire Regiment. He died on the same day as his great friend, Sid Weston.
Notes: Ernest Olive is commemorated by a plaque on the south wall of St Andrew's church in Countesthorpe.

WALTER CHARLES PEET

Rank: Corporal
Number: 504
Regiment, Corps etc:
4th Battalion, Leicestershire Regiment
Military Service:
Date and circumstances of Death:
Peet died at the 5th Northern General Hospital, Leicester on 2nd April 1916. His death certificate records the cause of death as cerebral abscess, following a gunshot wound to the face eight and a half months before.
Age: 33
Buried: Foston Road Cemetery, Countesthorpe (consecrated grave number 504)
Family: Walter was one of the five children of George Alfred Tilley and Harriet Peet. He was born in about 1884, a few years before the marriage of his parents in 1888. Walter himself married Harriett Burbage of Cosby at the parish church in Cosby on 13 September 1902. They had two children; Eva Eliza (baptised on 26 July 1904) and Alfred Sidney (baptised 18 January 1913). His widow died in 1965, at the age of 86, at 11 Conaglen Road, Leicester.

W.C. Peet's grave in Foston Road cemetery, Countesthorpe

WILLIAM SIMMS

Rank: Gunner
Number: 294919
Regiment, Corps etc:
147th Heavy Battery, Royal Garrison Artillery
Military Service: Simms served as a driver with the ammunition train of his battery. A letter to his mother, after his death, recorded that he was "a good lad and an excellent worker always looking after his horses well."
Date and circumstances of Death: Simms was killed as a result of a bombing raid on the horse lines, where he was working. He died on arrival at 1/2 East Lancashire Field Ambulance on 7 September 1917.
Age: 20
Buried: Brandhoek New Military Cemetery No. 3, 6.5 km west of Ypres, Belgium.
Family: William was the youngest child of Thomas Simms and his wife, Selena Lord. He had three sisters and a brother. He was unmarried.

Gunner William Simms

John Cawrey Soars

Rank: Private
Number: 23147
Regiment, Corps etc:
8th Battalion, Leicestershire Regiment
Military Service:
Date and circumstances of Death: John Soars died as a prisoner of war of the Germans, of influenza, on 12 June 1918
Age: 29
Buried: Cologne Southern Cemetery (grave e/f XIV.C.E)
Family: John was the son of Edward Soars and his wife, Minnie Kate Pollard, of Main Street, Countesthorpe. He had an elder sister, Augusta Elizabeth, born in 1885. John married Mary Isobel Harrold in 1908. They lived in Station Road, Countesthorpe and had three children: Edward (born in 1909) Kathleen (1910) and Harold John (1918).

Family group consisting of Augusta (sister), John, Isobel (wife), Edward (son), Edward (father), Minnie Kate (mother nee Pollard) and Kathleen (daughter).

Alfred William Stafford

Rank: Sergeant
Number: 424
Regiment, Corps etc: (Royal) Army Veterinary Corps
Military Service:
Date and circumstances of Death: Stafford died of valvular disease of the heart, combined with heart failure at the Rubery Temporary Military Hospital on 25 March 1919.
Age: c. 28
Buried: Countesthorpe, Foston Road Cemetery (Unconsecrated grave ref. 640)
Family: Alfred was the third child and only son of Alfred Stafford and Clare Able of Cosby - who were married at Peatling Parva on 23 March 1885. Alfred (junior) was born at Gilmorton. At the time of Alfred's death, his parents had moved from Gilmorton to Countesthorpe.
Notes: Alfred was employed as an engine cleaner before his military service.

Sjt A. W. Stafford's grave with its Commonwealth war graves headstone in Foston cemetery, Countesthorpe

HERBERT SWANN

Rank: Driver
Number:
Regiment, Corps etc:
Royal Field Artillery
Military Service: Swann seems to have been invalided out of the army in 1916 following an accident.
Date and circumstances of Death: Swann died at Foston Road, Countesthorpe on 2 November 1918. His death certificate gives the cause of his death as influenza but also records that he had paraplegia, following an injury to his spine. His sister Stella died the same day, also of influenza, and they were buried together. An endorsement to the only known photograph of Driver Swann records: *"Uncle Herbert had a gun carriage over him. He was leading driver. Fell off. Broke back. Night before he died he got out of bed at Countesthorpe and walked straight up. He and..."* [missing]
Age: 22
Buried: Countesthorpe Cemetery (unconsecrated number 636 – no headstone).

Driver Herbert Swann

Family: Herbert was the youngest of fourteen children of Frederick and Mary Ann Swann. His father was a shoemaker from Cossington. His mother came from North Kilworth.

Fred Thornton

Rank: Corporal
Number: 18611
Regiment, Corps etc:
8th Battalion, Leicestershire Regiment
Date and circumstances of Death:
Acting Corporal Thornton was killed on 3 May 1917, during the battle for Fontaine-les-Croisilles. His battalion, accompanied by two tanks (which soon broke down) went over the top in two waves, of two lines each, at 3.45 a.m. Advancing under cover of a creeping barrage, the 8th Leicesters swiftly lost their way in the pre-dawn darkness, dust and smoke. They ran into heavy resistance from the heavily defended Hindenburg Line and by 6.30 a.m. the attack was over. Corporal Thornton and over three hundred of his comrades had been killed and wounded.
Age: 23
Buried: Thornton is commemorated on the memorial at Arras (Bay 5) and on the war memorial in Saddington Parish Church.
Family: Fred was the eldest of nine children of Joseph Thornton, a hosiery factory manager, and his wife, Elizabeth Riddington. Both parents were born at Countesthorpe (where they also married) though Fred was born at Fleckney, where the family lived before a final move to Saddington. Joseph and Elizabeth Thornton are both buried in the churchyard at Saddington. Fred did not marry.

Corporal Fred Thornton

Joseph Henry Tilley

Rank: Private
Number: 801457
Regiment, Corps etc:
1/4th Battalion,
Leicestershire Regiment
Date and circumstances of Death:
Died 22 June 1917
Age: 26
Buried: Boulogne Eastern Cemetery, grave reference R/F IV.A.12
Family: Joseph was the son of George Alfred Tilley and Harriet Pect (the brother of Walter Charles Peet (who died at the 5th Northern General Hospital, Leicester. Joseph had a sister (Ann) and a brother (Thomas Edward). His mother died in giving birth to Thomas Edward, who was subsequently adopted by Philip and Sarah Ann Immins. Joseph Tilley did not marry.

Frank Veasey

Rank: Private
Number: SS/23110
Regiment, Corps etc:
2/6th Battalion,
South Staffordshire Regiment
Date and circumstances of Death:
Died 4 December 1917
Age: 20
Buried: Etaples Military cemetery, grave R/F XXXI A6A. He is also commemorated on the war memorial at South Wigston.
Family: Frank was the eldest child of Fred Veasey, a railway engine fireman, and his wife, Ada Riddington. Both Fred and Ada were born in Countesthorpe, where they also married. Frank was baptised at Countesthorpe on 14 February 1896. He had one brother (Harry – who is also recorded on the Countesthorpe memorial) and four sisters (Florrie, Edna, Beatrice, and Freda). By the time of the 1901 census, the family was living at number 8, Twenty Row, Wigston Magna.

HARRY VEASEY
Rank: Private
Number: 66757
Regiment, Corps etc:
1/5th Battalion,
Northumberland Fusiliers
Date and circumstances of Death:
Died 10 April 1918
Age: 18
Buried: Trois Arbres Cemetery, Steenwerck, III.D.1. He is also recorded on the South Wigston war memorial.
Family: The brother of Frank Veasey.

HUBERT VEASEY
Rank: Private
Number: 50508
Regiment, Corps etc: 2/5th Lancashire Fusiliers
Date and circumstances of Death: 10 November 1918
Age: c.19
Buried: Irchonwelz Communal Cemetery, Hainault, Belgium
Family: Hubert was the second of three sons of Joseph Henry Veasey and his wife, Lucy Riddington. In addition to his brothers (Thomas Henry and Albert Edward) Hubert also had a half-sister – Evelyn.

EDWIN CHARLES WALLIS
Rank: Private
Number: 14909
Regiment, Corps etc:
7th Battalion,
Leicestershire Regiment
Military Service: Edwin Wallis attested for military service at Leicester on 7 September 1914. He gave his age as 19 years and 150 days. He was 5 feet $10^{1}/_{8}$ inches tall and weighed 140 pounds. He had a 'fresh' complexion, grey eyes and auburn hair. After two months at the depot, where he was promoted to acting, unpaid lance corporal, he was posted to the 7th Battalion, Leicestershire Regiment on 31th October 1914. His surviving military papers include a report that he was admitted to hospital in January 1916 with burns to his hand from a 'starlight' flare pistol. His commanding officer certified that it was not a self-inflicted wound. He passed from 5 General Hospital at Rouen to the Etaples Base Hospital, before returning to his battalion on 27 May 1916.
Date and circumstances of Death: On 22th July 1916 he was first returned 'missing believed wounded' and then 'Killed in Action'. A week before the 7th Leicesters had been thrown into the attack on Bazentin-le-Petit Wood, near Mametz. The objective was

Edwin Charles & Horace Samuel Wallis

wife, Anna Maria Partridge. They were both natives of Kettering, Northants where Edwin was also born on 24th April 1895, at 115, Princess Street, Kettering. Samuel and Anna Wallis came to Countesthorpe as House Parents of Number 4 Cottage, at the Cottage Homes. Edwin did not marry.
Notes: Edwin Charles Wallis was employed, like his parents, as a school teacher.

reached but losses were severe (18 officers and 535 men) leaving barely 100 men to hold the newly acquired positions. It seems likely that Edwin Wallis died at Bazentin Wood but that his fate was not realised until the remnants of the battalion were pulled out of the front line and returned to billets at Moncheaux.
Age: 21
Buried: Thiepval Memorial, pier and face 2c and 3a.
Family: Edwin Wallis was the son of Samuel Wallis and his

Horace Samuel Wallis

Rank: Private
Number: 42489/42490
Regiment, Corps etc:
7th and 20th Battalions, Durham Light Infantry.
Military Service: Horace Wallis attested for military service on 22 March 1916. At the time he was living at 13, Glossop Street, Leicester and employed as a warehouseman. He gave his age as 18 years and 252 days. His height was recorded as 5 feet 4$^{7}/_{8}$inches and his chest (fully expanded) as 36 inches. On 6 September 1916 he was posted to the 15th Durham Light Infantry and allotted a new regimental number. He suffered difficulties with his feet, being admitted to hospital in France and then, on 9 March 1917, being invalided home on the hospital ship *Gloucester Castle*. In June 1917 he was returned to active service, joining the 20th Durham Light Infantry on 9 June 1917. On the last day of July 1917 he was posted 'missing'. His service papers, at the National Archives, include a plaintive letter of 15 August 1917, from his father to the officer in charge of Territorial Force records asking for news: "Will you be kind enough to inform me if my son (now in France) is enjoying good health, I am feeling most anxious

This composite picture, created after the death of both sons, shows Samuel & Anna Wallis and their sons Edwin Charles and Horace Samuel.

about him, as I have received no news from him for more than three weeks past he was then alright and in good health…" He had been dead for more than a fortnight.
Date and circumstances of Death:
31 July 1917
Age: 21
Buried: recorded on the Menin Gate, Ypres.
Family: Horace was the second son of Samuel and Anna Wallis and the brother of Edwin Charles Wallis. He was unmarried.
Notes: There is a story that Horace Wallis was profoundly deaf and therefore exempt military service but that he was presented with a white feather and so felt compelled to enlist.

Arthur Wells

Rank: Private
Number: 23251
Regiment, Corps etc:
2nd Battalion,
Leicestershire Regiment
Date and circumstances of Death:
23rd April 1917. At the time of Wells' death, the Leicesters were heavily engaged against Turkish positions along the River Tigris. The 23rd April saw the heaviest fighting, in which the battalion lost 21 officers and men killed and 105 wounded.
Age: c. 23
Buried: Not known. Wells is commemorated on the Basra War Memorial, Iraq.
Family: Arthur Wells was the son of William Wells, an agricultural labourer from Husbands Bosworth and his wife, Roseanna Meer, who was born in Ashby Parva. Arthur had one sister (Annie, who was born c. 1897 and died in 1903) and three brothers, Charles (born in Lutterworth, c. 1884) William T. (born in Mowsley, c. 1887) and James (born in Countesthorpe c. 1891).They were resident in Countesthorpe by the 1891 census.
Notes: Arthur wells, like three other Countesthorpe men killed in the Great War, was a member of the parish church choir.

Arthur Wells (left) photographed as part of the choir

SIDNEY WESTON

Rank: Private
Number: 242312
Regiment, Corps etc:
2/5th Battalion,
Leicestershire Regiment
Date and circumstances of Death:
26 September 1917. A story related by a friend, Arthur Burdett of Countesthorpe, tells how Weston was wounded in the leg and being carried back to safety on a stretcher, when a shell exploded nearby, killing him.
Age: 20
Buried: His name is recorded on the Tyne Cot Memorial, at Zonnebeke, West-Vlannderen, Belgium (panel 50-51)
Family: Sidney was the eldest son of William Weston and Martha Ann Gillam, his wife. He was born on 12 November 1897 at Countesthorpe. Sidney had a brother (Herbert) and three sisters (Dorothy, Mary Ellen and Maud). At the time of Sidney's death, the family were living at 25, Main Street, Countesthorpe. He was the uncle of Henrietta Schultka.
Notes: Sidney, like his father and brother, worked in the hosiery trade. He and his brother both played for the Countesthorpe football team.

Private Sidney Weston

Albert Ernest Yorke

Rank: Corporal
Number: 2010
Regiment, Corps etc:
1/5th Battalion,
Manchester Regiment
Date and circumstances of Death:
7th August 1915
Age: 27
Buried: His name is recorded on the Cape Helles Memorial, Turkey
Family: Albert Ernest was born on 18th March 1888, the son of William John York (no 'e') and his wife, Mary Bronton. His father was a press man, in the boot and shoe trade, resident at 70, Argyle Street, Leicester. The 1891 census shows that he had two sisters, Louisa and May. His father came from Daventry, Northants., while his mother came from Whalpool Marsh, Lincs. There may be a link with the York family of Countesthorpe, as they originated in Northamptonshire too.

Frederick York

Rank: Private
Number: 25828
Regiment, Corps etc:
1st Battalion,
Leicestershire Regiment
Date and circumstances of Death:
Died 15 September 1916
Age: 30
Buried: His name is on the Thiepval Memorial.
Family: Frederick was the second son (of three brothers and two sisters) of John York and his wife, Emily Riddington. He was born about 1886.

Private Fredrick York (middle of second row)

THE GREAT WAR
KILBY'S WAR DEAD

THOMAS HAINES
Rank: Lance-corporal
Number: 23170
Regiment, Corps etc:
21st Battalion,
Machine Gun Corps
Date and circumstances of Death:
Died 24 March 1918
Age: 23
Buried: Commemorated on the Pozieres Memorial, Panels 90-93. His name is also recorded on the war memorial in St Andrew's Church, Peatling Parva.
Family: Thomas was one of the four children (three sons and one daughter) of Edward Haines (of Ragdale) and his wife, Sarah Jane Mears (born in Thurlaston). In 1901 Edward Haines was living at Shawell, working as a domestic gardener.
Notes: Thomas's brothers both served during the Great War; William with 41st Battery, 2nd Brigade, Royal Field Artillery and John with the 8th Leicesters. Both survived.

CHARLES HASSELL
Rank: Private
Number: 9/13729
Regiment, Corps etc:
7th Battalion The Queen's (Royal West Surrey) Regiment
Date and circumstances of Death:
Died 18 November 1918
Age: 29
Buried: Aveluy Communal cemetery, Extension: M. 48
Family: Charles was the eldest child of John Hassell (a baker) and his wife, Elizabeth Asher. They had married at Kilby church in 1885 and had two sons and three daughters, all born in the village.
Notes: Charles Hassell married Mary Green, of Stoke Albany, at Sibbertoft, Northamptonshire, on 10 February 1913. Charles was then working as a gardener at Sibbertoft.

Main Street, Kilby looking East c. 1905

John Abbott Pask
Rank: Private
Number: 20576
Regiment, Corps etc:
9th Battalion, Leicestershire Regiment
Date and circumstances of Death: Died 16 July 1916
Age: 23
Buried: Flat Iron Copse Cemetery, Mametz. Grave R/F XI B 5.
Family: John was the son of John Pask, from Nocton, Lincs., a shepherd employed on the Wistow Hall estate, and his wife, Annie, who was born at Monks Kirby, Warwickshire. The Pasks had seven sons and four daughters, all born at Kilby. The family lived in the Kilby Lodge Cottages, Fleckney Road, Kilby.

Frank Wormleighton
Rank: Corporal
Number: 50255
Regiment, Corps etc:
10th Battalion, Lancashire Fusiliers
Date and circumstances of Death: Died 25 August 1918
Age: 20
Buried: Wormleighton is commemorated on the memorial at Vis-en-Artois, Pas de Calais, Panels 5 and 6.
Family: Frank was one of the nine children (five sons and four daughters) of William and Sarah Ann Wormleighton. William was employed as a gardener (not domestic). Both were born in Leicester.

Main Street, Kilby looking West c. 1905

THE GREAT WAR
PEATLING MAGNA'S WAR DEAD

WHITE CHESTERTON
Rank: Private
Number: 118046
Regiment, Corps etc:
1/3rd Sherwood Foresters
(Notts & Derbys)
Date and circumstances of Death:
Died 17 October 1918
Age: 19
Buried: Fresnoy-le-Grand Communal Cemetery Extension
Family: White was the youngest son of Thomas Chesterton, a farmer, from Earl Shilton, and his wife, Mary Ann, from Sutton-in-the-Elms. Thomas Chesterton was a tenant farmer, moving from Thringston, to Bilson and then Smeeton Westerby. At the time of White's death, the family were farming at Lower Brookhill Farm, Peatling Magna, as tenants of Trinity College, Cambridge. Although both White's parents died at Peatling Magna, they are buried at Countesthorpe Foston Road Cemetery, their headstone including White's name.

HENRY COOK(E)
Rank: Lance-corporal
Number: 7125
Regiment, Corps etc:
1st Battalion,
Leicestershire Regiment
Date and circumstances of Death:
Died 18 December 1914
Age: 29
Buried: Commemorated on the Ploegstert Memorial
Family: Henry Cook(e) was the illegitimate son of Elizabeth Cook(e), born in the Lutterworth workhouse in 1885. The 1881 census shows Elizabeth Cook(e) at the age of 16, working as a domestic servant for Ernest Bates in St Margaret's, Leicester. In 1887 Cook(e)'s mother married Simeon Hubbard, of Willoughby Waterless. Hubbard died in 1896, leaving Elizabeth a widow, with three more children. By 1901 Henry was working as a farm servant to Mr Warren at Westfield House, Arnesby.

ALLEN MARSHALL

Rank: Private
Number: 27034
Regiment, Corps etc:
9th Battalion,
Leicestershire Regiment
Military Service: Marshall attested for military service on 29th November 1915. He was posted to the 12th Leicesters on 3 April 1916 for basic training, before joining the British Expeditionary Force at the end of July 1916. He served briefly with the 8th Leicesters until he was wounded in his left forearm and left foot. Marshall was treated at Rouen before being evacuated home on 28 September 1916.
He spent from 31 October 1916 until 15 December 1916 at the Command depot Hospital at Ripon. He returned to active service with the 9th Leicesters on the last day of May 1917.
Date and circumstances of Death: He died of wounds received in action on 30 October 1917.
Age: 26
Buried: Lijssenthoek Military Cemetery, Belgium. XXI.DD.11

Family: Alan Marshall was the illegitimate son of Clara Marshall, a domestic servant. He was born on 21 April 1890, at Peatling Magna. On 21 November 1914 Allen married Evelyn Florence Knight of Bruntingthorpe. Their son, Wilfred Sidney, was born on 5 June 1915. At the time of his marriage, Allen was working as a gardener, though on his enlistment he described himself as a tram conductor.

Edward James Tilley

Rank: Private
Number: 29748
Regiment, Corps etc:
14th Battalion,
Worcestershire Regiment
Date and circumstances of Death:
Died 5 February 1917
Age: 38
Buried: Commemorated on the Thiepval Memorial: Pier and Face 5A and 6C
Family: Edward was the youngest son of William Tilley, of Burton Overy, and his wife, Elizabeth Hubbard, who was born at Willoughby Waterless. Edward had a twin sister, Ada Jane, and six other siblings; four brothers (William Thomas, George Richard, John Thomas and Lewis Hubbard) and two sisters (Mary Ann and Elizabeth Maria). Edward was not married. Edward James was born at Peatling Magna.

Private Edward James Tilley

WILLIAM EDWARD TILLEY
Rank: Private
Number: 21973
Regiment, Corps etc: 4th Battalion, Grenadier Guards
Military Service: William E. Tilley attested at Nuneaton, for the Grenadier Guards at the age of nineteen, on 11 January 1915. He exceeded the minimum requirements, the form completed by a civil surgeon, W. S. Nason, recording that Tilley was 6 feet 2¼ inches tall, weighed 177lbs and had a chest of 41 inches (when expanded). He had a fresh complexion, brown hair and eyes, and could be distinguished by a scar on his left forearm. The Statement of Service is sadly lacking in detail, recording only that Tilley joined his regiment at Caterham on 14 January 1915 and died from wounds received in action on 1 August 1917. His next of kin were notified a week later.
Age: c. 21
Buried: Dozinghem Military Cemetery, Belgium.
Family: William was one of the two sons (William and Horace) and six daughters (Alice, Ada, Maud Annie, Mary Ellen, Grace Evelyn and Margaret Hannah) of William Thomas Tilley and his wife, Jane Thurn. William

Private William Edward Tilley

Thomas Tilley was a native of Peatling Magna. His wife was born at Anstey in Warwickshire. By 1901 W. T. Tilley was farming at WilloughbyWaterless, though he later moved to Nuneaton.
Notes: William was the nephew of Edward James Tilley

The Great War
Peatling Parva's war dead

THOMAS GLENN
Rank: Private
Number: 242165
Regiment, Corps etc:
South Staffordshire Regiment
Military Service: Tom Glenn was employed as a baker in the army.
Date and circumstances of Death: Private Glenn died after a six month illness, at the Isolation Hospital, Gilrose, Leicester, of pulmonary tuberculosis.
Age: 20
Buried: Welford Road Cemetery, Leicester.
Family: Tom was born on 10th December 1898, at Syston in Lincolnshire, where his father, James Glenn, was employed as a farm waggoner. Presumably he also worked at some time at Peatling Parva, though no record of this has been found.
Notes: Tom's mother, Eliza Castle Glenn (née Smith) and his brother, Charles Sydney, are also buried at the Welford Road Cemetery.

THOMAS HAINES
Lance-corporal Haines is listed on both the Peatling Parva and Kilby War Memorials. See page 44.

THOMAS LEE
Regiment, Corps etc:
Leicestershire Yeomanry
Military Service: Thomas is known to have enlisted in the Leicestershire Yeomanry by 1906.
Family: Thomas was the eldest son of Stephen Lee, a butcher and grazier and his wife, Fanny Measures. He was born at Peatling Parva in 1881. He had three sisters (Alice Measures, Eliza, and Agnes) and two brothers (Percy and Joseph). At the time of the 1901 census, Thomas was living at Peatling Parva with his parents, working as a butcher.

W PHILLIPS
Family: Possibly the son of George and Ann Phillips, farmers at Hall Farm, Peatling Parva.

HERBERT PRENTICE

Rank: Private
Number: M2/269735
Regiment, Corps etc:
880th Motor Transport Company, Army Service Corps
Date and circumstances of Death:
18 October 1918.
Age: 31
Buried: Skopje British Cemetery, Balkans
Family: Herbert was one of nine children of George H. Prentice, an agricultural labourer, born in Warwick, and his wife, Catherine Bingley, from Peatling Parva. Of his brothers (Frederick, Andrew, Francis John, and Joseph) one, Frederick, had seen service with the Imperial Yeomanry during the South African War, dying of enteric fever at Thabanchu on 17 December 1901. Herbert had four sisters: Kate, Annie Elizabeth, Alice and Amy.

Herbert married Emily Lorinda, the daughter of Henry Cheney (a farmer) on 15 August 1915, at St Mary's, Bruntingthorpe. At the time his occupation was given as 'chauffeur', which accounts presumably for his service with the motor transport of the ASC.

War Memorial 1914-1918, St Andrew's Church, Peatling Parva

JASPER CHARLES STEWART

Rank: Private
Number: 50604
Regiment, Corps etc:
10th Battalion, Cheshire Regiment
Military Service: Stewart attested for military service at Leicester on 17 January 1916, being posted to the Army reserve on the same day. He was mobilised on 7 June that year, reporting to the depôt of the Leicestershire Regiment at Glen Parva. After a few days, on 11 June, Stewart was posted to the 3rd Battalion, Leicestershire Regiment for his initial training. On 2 March 1917 he received orders to join the 1st Battalion of the Leicesters at the front. He embarked at Folkestone the next day but shortly after his arrival in France, on 19 March he was posted instead to the 10th Cheshires.
Date and circumstances of Death:
Private Stewart was reported missing on 1 August 1917.
Age: 29
Buried: Divisional Collecting Post Cemetery and Extension, Ypres (Ieper) II.F.11
Family: Jasper was born in Berwick-upon-Tweed. His attestation papers show that by 1916 his father was dead, his mother being recorded as Helen Stewart. He had two brothers (Daniel and George, aged 41 and 35 respectively) and a 43 year-old sister, Mrs Ellen Wright. All were resident in Scotland. Jasper had married Georgina Barkley McIntyre in Fife, Scotland, on 11 April 1913. They had three children (Jasper Charles born 29 March 1914, Catherine Helen, born 13 September 1915 and Isabell Margaret, born 18 November 1917).
Notes: Jasper Stewart was employed as a gardener by Colonel William Alexander Stewart Gemmell, at Peatling Parva Hall.

George Alfred Tarratt

Rank: Private
Number: 11502
Regiment, Corps etc: 2nd Battalion, Leicestershire Regiment
Military Service: George Tarratt enlisted in the army on 11th August 1914; a week after the declaration of war. He undertook his recruit's training with the 3rd Leicesters at the Glen Parva depôt, before embarkation at Southampton, on 19th March 1915, to join the 2nd Battalion, Leicestershire Regiment.
Date and circumstances of Death: On 29th May 1915 he was reported as missing after 'operations in the field'. On 25th March 1916 his death was officially certified.
Age: At the time of his enlistment, Tarratt's age was recorded as 17 years and 92 days.
Buried: Tarratt's body, as the delay between his being reported missing and certified dead suggests, was not recovered. His name is recorded on the Memorial at Le Touret. He is also remembered on war memorials at Peatling Parva and Botcheston.
Family: George A. Tarratt was the son of George Tarratt, who kept the Plough public house at Bruntingthorpe, until his death in 1901. His mother, Harriett, remarried and, by the time of her son's death, was Mrs Harriet Chown, living at the Industrial School Cottages, Desford.
Notes: George Tarratt's medical history shows that he was employed before the war as a labourer. He was only 5 feet and 3½ inches tall, with a 32 inch chest and a weight of 112 lbs.

WILLIAM WOODWARD
Rank: Private
Number: 24332
Regiment, Corps etc:
1st Battalion, Grenadier Guards
Date and circumstances of Death:
Died 25 September 1916
Age: 26
Buried: Peronne Road Cemetery, I. E. 18
Family: William was the eldest of the four children of Samuel Woodward and his wife, Mary Mears. All were born at Thurlaston. By the 1901 census, Samuel Woodward was dead and Mary had remarried and was living with her new husband, Edwin Jones, at Stretton Parva. With them were Samuel's children (William, Job, Daisy Ellen and Walter) and their half-brother, Edwin Jones, aged one year. The family later moved to Peatling Parva. William Woodward himself married on 14 May 1916, at Lubenham Parish church. He was already a Grenadier Guardsman, resident at Chelsea Barracks, while his bride, Fanny, was the daughter of Joseph Bird of Lubenham. At the time of William's death, Fanny was resident at 33, Orange Street, South Wigston. She did not remarry.

THE GREAT WAR
SHEARSBY'S WAR DEAD

Lionel Sidney Burton

Rank: Sergeant
Number: 1543
Regiment, Corps etc:
'B' Squadron, 1/1st Leicestershire Yeomanry
Date and circumstances of Death:
Died 13 May 1915
Age: 26
Buried: His name is recorded on the Menin Gate, Ypres
Family: Lionel was one of two sons of H. H. Burton, the jeweller, of 116, Granby Street, Leicester. Lionel was reported to have married his former secretary, Lillie, two days before his departure for the front. She later married a Charles Hulls, moving to Ickenham near Uxbridge, Middlesex.
Notes: Lionel Burton worked in the hosiery trade. He was well known as a rugby player, joining the Leicester Rugby Football Club for three seasons as a forward.

Sergeant Lionel Burton

WILLIAM CLOWES

Rank: Private
Number: 15659
Regiment, Corps etc:
7th Battalion,
Leicestershire Regiment
Military Service: William Clowes enlisted on 15 October 1914. Following a period of initial training at Glen Parva, he was posted on 7 November 1914 to the 7th Battalion, Leicestershire Regiment. After further training at Aldershot and on Salisbury Plain, Clowes embarked, with his battalion, at Southampton, for France on 29 July 1915. His fatal wound was received, presumably, in the fighting along the Hindenburg Line in the spring and summer of 1917. By the end of July 1917 Clowes' battalion was exhausted and was pulled out of the line to form part of the divisional reserve.
Date and circumstances of Death:
Died 25 July 1917
Age: 40
Buried: Croisilles British Cemetery, Pas de Calais R/F I.G. 4
Family: William was one of eight children of William Clowes and his wife Millicent Shuttlewood, who had married at Shearsby on 5 December 1864. The 1881 census shows the family living at The Bank, Shearsby and records William's siblings as Harry, Martha, Namey, Charles, Millicent, Anne and Bertie. At his death, Clowes' personal effects were returned to his sister, Mrs Annie Tipping, at Shearsby.
Notes: William Clowes' attestation papers records that he was 5 feet 6½ inches tall, weighed 133 pounds and had a chest of 36½ inches (with an expansion of 2 inches). Bertie Clowes, who served with the Canadian forces, is also recorded on the Roll of Honour in Shearsby Church.

HORACE ALFRED HENSMAN

Rank: Private
Number: 13015
Regiment, Corps etc:
7th Battalion, Bedfordshire Regiment
Military Service:
Date and circumstances of Death:
1 July 1916
Age: 19
Buried: Dantzig Alley British Cemetery, Mametz, Grave III, D.5.
Family: Horace Hensman was born on 27 July 1896, at lower Thrift Street, Northampton. He was the eldest son of Alfred Hensman and his wife Angelina Jane Jenkins. Alfred Hensman was born in Ecton, Northants. Angelina Jenkins came from Northampton. They presumably met while working as attendants at the Lunatic Asylum in Northampton.
Horace had at least one brother, Percy Harold George Hensman, born in 1900. Percy also served in the army, enlisting under-age on 16 October 1915. Percy's service records survive at the National Archives and show Lena Hensman as his next of kin, keeping the Old Crown Inn at Shearsby. Both Alfred and 'Lena Hensman are buried at Shearsby in the churchyard.

Private Horace Alfred Herbert Hensman

ROBERT SIMONS
Rank: Private
Number: 21373
Regiment, Corps etc: Coldstream Guards
Date and circumstances of Death: Died 13 April 1918
Age: 31
Buried: Robert Simons is recorded on the Ploegsteert Memorial, Panel 1
Family: Robert was the son of Reuben Simons and his wife, Eliza Weston, who married at Shearsby on 1 July 1872. They had at least six children: Richard, Charles, Robert, Mary Elizabeth and Florence Rebecca. Robert Simons married – his wife, Grace, being noted by the Commonwealth War Graves Commission as resident at 103, St Leonard's Road, Clarendon Park, Leicester.

J S WATTS
Rank: Gunner
Number: 26481
Regiment, Corps etc: Royal Garrison Artillery
Date and circumstances of Death: 22 June 1916
Buried: Baghdad (North Gate) War Cemetery, Iraq, ref. XIV. K. 11

Memorial at Ploegsteert cemetery, Belgium

The Second World War
Countesthorpe's war dead

JOHN PATRICK BARRETT

Rank: Pilot Sergeant
Number: 1230355
Regiment, Corps etc:
122 Squadron, (Volunteer Reserve) Royal Air Force
Military Service: At the time of Pilot Sergeant Barrett's death, his squadron was based at Hornchurch. The squadron was equipped with Spitfires, flying sweeps across northern France.
Date and circumstances of Death:
Died 19 June 1942
Age: 20

Buried: Brookwood Military Cemetery, near Pirbright, Surrey.
Family: John Barrett was the son of John Gordon Barrett and his wife, Angela Mary. The family lived at Thornleigh, Foston Road, Countesthorpe.

Thornleigh, Foston Road, Countesthorpe

Robert Sidney Brothwell

Number: 1238487
Regiment, Corps etc:
Royal Air Force Volunteer Reserve
Military Service: Brothwell enlisted in the RAF(VR) in March 1941. He was exempt compulsory military service due to his agricultural work but was determined to qualify as a fighter pilot. In February 1942 he was posted to Canada (and later the USA) for further training. He returned to the UK in November 1942 and was promoted to Flight Sergeant. Although qualified in night flying, Brothwell was disappointed to be sent to a training unit as an instructor, rather than to an operational unit.
Date and circumstances of Death: Brothwell was killed on 20th August 1943, at Stock Farm, Chorley, Cheshire, when his student pilot lost control of their aeroplane.
Age: 21
Buried: Commonwealth War Grave, Countesthorpe Cemetery
Family: Robert was the son of Wilfred and Florence Brothwell, both from Thurlby, near Bourne in Lincolnshire. He had three sisters; Eileen, Jean and Margaret. Wilfred and Florence were married at Knighton in 1919, where Florence was employed as housekeeper

Flight Sergeant Robert Sidney Brothwell

by the vicar. Wilfred Brothwell worked as a market gardener, in 1933 moving to his own market garden at the Vineries, Station Road, Countesthorpe.
Notes: Robert (Bob) Brothwell attended school in Countesthorpe where he was an able student, establishing a school garden, playing in the school football team, and winning a national writing competition. He also won a scholarship to the agricultural college at Sutton Bonnington.

DOUGLAS ARTHUR CHAPMAN

Rank: Private
Number: 7674382
Regiment, Corps etc:
Royal Army Pay Corps
Date and circumstances of Death:
Douglas Chapman took his own life, by gas poisoning, on the evening of Sunday, 26 April 1942, while his widowed mother was at Evensong at St Andrew's church.
Age: 24
Buried: Foston Road Cemetery, Countesthorpe
Family: Douglas was the only son of John Alfred Chapman (who died during the Great War) and his wife, Sarah Cox. He was not married.
Notes: Douglas was educated in Countesthorpe and at the Wyggeston Boys' Grammar School, before joining a firm of solicitors.

Young Douglas with his mother, Sarah

JOHN KEITH CHAPMAN

Rank: Private
Number: 14714124
Regiment, Corps etc:
1st Battalion
Leicestershire Regiment
Date and circumstances of Death:
Died 8 October 1944
Age: 18
Buried: Baarle-Nassau Roman Catholic Churchyard. He is commemorated by a stained glass window in the north wall of St Andrew's Church, Countesthorpe.
Family: John Chapman was the son of Samuel Arthur and Linda Louise Chapman. He had three sisters; Christine, Valerie and Mary.
Notes: John was educated at the Church School in Main Street, Countesthorpe, and then at the secondary school in Bassett Street, South Wigston. He worked then for the family building firm.

HENRY ERNEST CREASEY

Rank: Leading Aircraftsman
Number: 1304130
Regiment, Corps etc:
Royal Air Force
(Volunteer Reserve)
Date and circumstances of Death:
Henry Creasey collapsed and died whilst helping to put out a rick fire at College Farm, Bearley in Warwickshire, on 15th May 1943. An inquest later determined that the death was due to sclerosis of the coronary arteries, which had been aggravated by military service.
Age: 35
Buried: Foston Road Cemetery, Countesthorpe (grave number 710; unconsecrated, east side).
Family: Henry was married with two children. His wife, Kay, and two children (Michael and Patricia) had come from London as evacuees. They lived on Waterloo Crescent, Countesthorpe but returned to London at Henry Creasey's death.

Leading Aircraftsman Henry Ernest Creasey Buried at Foston Road cemetery, Countesthorpe

LESLIE ERNEST CUTLER

Rank: Trooper
Number: 7954784
Regiment, Corps etc:
3rd County of London Yeomanry (Sharpshooters); Royal Armoured Corps
Date and circumstances of Death: Killed in action on 5 October 1943.
Age: 21
Buried: Sangro River War Cemetery, Italy
Family: Leslie (always known as Roger - as he disliked his given names) was the son of Percy James Cutler and his wife. He had two sisters (Grace and Edna) and two brothers (Jack and Edgar).

At the time of his death the family lived at 9 Holywell Road, Aylestone.
Notes: 'Roger' Cutler was educated at the village school and later worked at Clarke's Farm, Willoughby Road, Countesthorpe.

Station Road, Countesthorpe

THOMAS LEONARD FIELDING
Rank: Private
Number: 10532054
Regiment, Corps etc:
4th Ordnance Store Company,
Royal Army Ordnance Corps
Military Service: Private Fielding's active military service was brief. Sent with reinforcements to Singapore, Fielding's ship docked just as the island surrendered to the Japanese. He was a prisoner-of-war even before he reached dry land.
Date and circumstances of Death: Fielding died in a cholera epidemic (one of three hundred) at Nieke Camp, on 16th August 1943.
Age: 23
Buried: The bodies of the victims of cholera at Nieke were cremated and the ashes interred at Kanchanaburi War Cemetery, Thailand. Thomas Fielding is also remembered on his parents' gravestone at Foston churchyard and on the memorial in Countesthorpe church.
Family: Thomas was born on 26 September 1926, the eldest child of Herbert Henry Fielding (of Houghton on the Hill) and his wife, Miriam Knight (whose parents worked Hurst's farm, Newton Harcourt). Thomas had a brother (Maurice) and a sister (Josephine). The family lived at 'Ivydene', 39 Station Road, Countesthorpe. He

Private Thomas Leonard Fielding

attended a small private school in Countesthorpe run by a Miss Yemm and later moved on to the Wyggeston Boys' School, Leicester. He left school at the age of 17, taking a job with the State Assurance Company in Leicester.

Victor Clarence Fretter

Rank: Sergeant
Number: 75138
Regiment, Corps etc:
220 squadron, Royal Air Force (Volunteer Reserve)
Military Service: Sergeant Fretter joined the RAFVR on 31 May 1939. He had been employed as an aircraft fitter at Armstrong Siddeley in Coventry and so already had valuable experience. He was promoted to sergeant having trained as a wireless operator/air gunner. At the beginning of 1942 Fretter's squadron had moved to Nutts Corner in Northern Ireland, from where its Fortress IIA aircraft were flown on anti-shipping patrols over the North Atlantic.
Date and circumstances of Death: Sergeant Fretter died on 10 August 1942 as a result of an aircraft accident. His death certificate records that he died from multiple injuries and severe burns caused in a 'plane crash.
Age: 23
Buried: Sergeant Fretter was buried at the Frowlesworth Road Cemetery, Broughton Astley. His coffin was sent from Northern Ireland at government expense, accompanied by three wreaths - from the officers, sergeants and men of his squadron respectively.

Sergeant Victor Clarence Fretter

Family: Victor Fretter was the son of Clarence George Fretter, who had died as a prisoner of war in November 1918, and Mildred Jane Hubbard his wife. He had one sister, Violet.
Notes: Victor married Joan Munns on 6 February 1941. Their daughter, Patricia Ann, was born on 19 July 1942. A letter survives from Victor to his wife, asking her to arrange Patricia Ann's christening at the beginning of September, as he was due leave then and would be able to come home.

THOMAS CHARLES HILL

Rank: Gunner
Number: 11002061
Regiment, Corps etc:
195 Coast Battery, Royal Artillery
Date and circumstances of Death:
Thomas Hill died at home, in Countesthorpe, having been discharged from the army with cancer.
Age: 35
Buried: Foston Road Cemetery, Countesthorpe

Family: Thomas was one of the fourteen children (four of whom died in infancy) of Roland Hill and his wife, Susan Mary Koch. Susan Koch was born in South Africa in 1877, the daughter of a Boer and a 'Cape Coloured' wife. Thomas was born at Whetstone in 1910. He married Frances Page of Countesthorpe, at the Countesthorpe Methodist Church on 30 January 1937. They had one child; a daughter named Veronica.

Thomas (far left) with his family outside their home on Paradise Row, Blaby

Gwilym Rhys Hughes

Rank: Sergeant
Number: 7520121
Regiment, Corps etc:
Royal Army Medical Corps
Date and circumstances of Death:
Gwilym Hughes died as a result of a collision between his motor cycle and an army 'bus at the Morton Turn, Morton in Lugg, Herefordshire.
Age: 24
Buried: Llanfairfechan, North Wales
Family: Gwilym Hughes was the son of John and Bertha Hughes of Llanfairfechan. He was married to Doris Ruth Barklem on 6 October 1939 at the Register Office in Bangor. They had one son; Elwyn Rhys Hughes, born in 1940. At the time of her husband's death Doris was living at 109, Knighton Lane, Leicester. She moved later to a cottage in Green Lane, Countesthorpe but on her remarriage in 1945, moved again to Arnesby.

Sergeant Gwilym Rhys Hughes Buried in Llanfairfechan cemetery, North Wales

LARRAD LIONEL THOMAS JOSEPH LUCAS

Rank: Signalman
Number: 5332203
Regiment, Corps etc: Royal Corps of Signals, attached to the 8th Royal Tank Regiment, Royal Armoured Corps
Date and circumstances of Death: Larrad Lucas died on 25 November 1941.
Age: 33
Buried: Knightsbridge War Cemetery, Acroma, Libya (12. H. 13). A cemetery created in one of the Allied strong points for the defence of Tobruk and into which the bodies of soldiers who had died throughout Libya were later gathered.
Family: Larrad was the eldest son of Francis Henry Lucas and his wife, Dora June Pegg. Francis was born in about 1880 at Cairnscross, Gloucestershire. Dora was born at Blaby. They married at the church of St Thomas the Apostle, South Wigston in 1907. Francis Henry was serving in the army (presumably at Glen Parva) at the time, though he had previously been employed as a butcher. Francis and Dora had three sons, all of whom served during the war. Larrad was himself married, to Nora – of Ward End, Birmingham.
Notes: A notice of Larrad's death in the Leicester Chronicle states that he left a wife and child. It describes him as 'Leonard' the son of Francis Henry and the late Mrs Lucas, of the Bull's Head, Countesthorpe.

Ronald Henry Mason

Rank: Sapper
Number: 4841945
Regiment, Corps etc: 994 Docks Operating Company, Royal Engineers
Military Service: Although little is known of his military service, Ronald Mason was one of a trio of Countesthorpe men who met, by coincidence, on the dockside at Algiers prior to the invasion of Sicily in June 1943. The other two were J. R. Joyce and Frank Hickford.
Date and circumstances of Death: Ronald Mason died in the Mediterranean in June 1943. His death at sea was witnessed by Able Seaman J. R. Joyce.
Age: 27
Buried: Ronald is commemorated on the memorial at Brookwood.
Family: Ronald was the son of George Edwin Mason and his wife, Rosetta Gibbins. He had one brother (Gordon) and three sisters (Ida, Eva, and Rosetta – known as Ettie). The family were in Countesthorpe by 1913, living in Green Lane, but later moved to 5, Main Street, where George Mason grazed cattle and worked as a milkman. Ronald married Hilda Taylor and they had one daughter, Patricia. Hilda later remarried and moved to Fleetwood in Lancashire.

Sapper Ronald Henry Mason

Notes: Before joining the army, Ronald worked as a drayman for the Midland Railway.

Dennis Frederic Moore

Rank: Lance-corporal
Number: 7951476
Regiment, Corps etc:
7th Battalion, Royal West Kent Regiment (The Buffs); 141st Royal Armoured Corps
Military Service: Dennis Moore was a tank driver.
Date and circumstances of Death: From family knowledge it seems that Dennis was killed in action, dying in his tank on 14th September 1944.
Age: 21
Buried: Bayeux War Cemetery, France
Family: Dennis was the son of Edward Dennis Moore and his wife, Gertrude Lillie Trigg, who had married at St Mark's, Leicester, on 4 July 1916. Dennis was born on 24 December 1922. He had one sister, Kathleen, who married James Lord and still lives in Countesthorpe. The Moores had moved to Countesthorpe when Dennis was four, living on Waterloo Crescent and then Willoughby Road.
Notes: Dennis was educated at the school on Main Street and later worked for the Co-op Butchery department at Blaby. His great friend was Leslie Ernest (Roger) Cutler, who also died during the war.

Lance-corporal Dennis Frederic Moore

LEONARD NORTON

Rank: Lance-corporal
Number: 7908419
Regiment, Corps etc:
6th Battalion, Queen's Own Royal West Kent Regiment
Date and circumstances of Death:
Died 19 November 1943
Age: 23
Buried: Sangro River War Cemetery, Italy
Family: Leonard was the son of Henry and Emma Norton. Little is known of the family, except that they lived briefly on Waterloo Crescent, and that Leonard is believed to have had a sister called Eunice and two brothers; one of whom was named Albert.
Notes: Leonard attended the school in Main Street and played for the school football team in the mid 1930s.

Leonard Norton pictured as a member of the 1933-4 Main Street School football team

John Parsons

Rank: Flying Officer
Number: 124756
Regiment, Corps etc: 50 Squadron, Royal Air Force (Volunteer Reserve)
Military Service: At the time of Flying Officer Parsons' death, 50 Squadron was flying Lancaster bombers on raids over occupied France, Germany and Italy.
Date and circumstances of Death: Died 3 April 1943
Age: 27
Buried: John Parsons is commemorated on the memorial at Runnymede.

Family: John was the son of Walter William Parsons and his wife, Rosina Parker. When they were married at Wandsworth Register Office on 22nd August 1901, Walter Parsons gave his occupation as butler. Though John seems never to have lived in Countesthorpe, his sister, Helen Annie (born *c.* 1904) was employed as a teacher at the school in Main Street, and in 1956 married a retired headmaster, A. E. Shuttlewood.

Main Street School, Countesthorpe

HARRY RIDDINGTON

Rank: Private
Number: 11253680
Regiment, Corps etc:
'D' Company, 30th Battalion, Somerset Light Infantry
Military Service: Private Riddington served in Algiers and Italy.
Date and circumstances of Death: Harry Riddington was admitted to the 104 British General Hospital in Rome on 13 July 1945, suffering from pain and loss of use of his limbs. The illness was diagnosed as infective polyneuritis and he was placed on the dangerously ill list. The paralysis spread to his brain stem and Harry died at 3.30 on the afternoon of 18th July 1945. Letters from his company commander and nursing staff attest to his qualities as a soldier and patient.
Age: 44
Buried: Harry was buried in the Rome Military cemetery at 11 a.m. on Friday 20th July 1945.
Family: Harry was the eldest son of Horace Riddington and his wife, Louisa Lines. He had two brothers, Arthur and Anthony. Harry married Maud Measures on 26 September 1926. They had a daughter, Eveline Mary and worked together at Tompkins' hosiery factory on Station Road, Countesthorpe.

Private Harry Riddington

Notes: Both Harry and his wife had attended the village school and sang in the church choirs at Foston and Countesthorpe.

NORMAN ALFRED SMITH

Rank: Flight Sergeant
Number: 1578116
Regiment, Corps etc:
45 (Reserve) Squadron
Royal Air Force
Military Service: Norman Smith enlisted in the RAF in 1940. He trained as a navigator and wireless operator and was posted to number 45 Squadron. From 1942 the squadron was based in India and Burma, flying Vengeance dive-bombers and then Mosquitoes.
Date and circumstances of Death: Flight-Sergeant Smith was killed when the jeep, in which he and three others were travelling, overturned. The vehicle ran off the road and rolled on top of Norman Smith, killing him. The others survived.
Age: 22
Buried: Smith was buried first at Silchar Cemetery, India but in 1952, following new arrangements for the care of War Graves in India and Pakistan, the body was moved and reburied at the Gauhati War Cemetery, Assam, India: Plot IV, Row F, Grave number 6.

Flight Sergeant Nornam Alfred Smith

Family: Norman Smith was born at Countesthorpe on 8 September 1922. He was the second of the three children of Luke Smith and his wife, Naomi Cox. He had an older sister (Kathleen) and a younger brother (Arnold). His father had served as a military policeman during the Great War and returned to Countesthorpe to work as a hosiery warehouseman at Tompkins' factory.

THOMAS FRANK SPIBY

Rank: Leading Aircraftsman
Number: 749041
Regiment, Corps etc:
Royal Air Force
(Volunteer Reserve)
Date and circumstances of Death:
Thomas Spiby died at the Connaught Hospital, Farnborough. He had suffered a broken neck when a truck accidentally overturned.
Age: 29
Buried: Welford Road Cemetery, Leicester.
Family: Thomas was the son of Cecil Spiby, of 25 Medway Street, Leicester. He was a printer by trade. On 9th July 1938 Thomas married Constance Irene Lee, the daughter of Joseph Lee of Countesthorpe. The family settled at 27, Waterloo Crescent, Countesthorpe, where they had a son, Roger, born on 15th January 1939. Constance Spiby later remarried and moved to Whetstone.
Notes: Thomas Spiby was a keen bell-ringer, ringing at St Thomas's, South Wigston.

Leading Aircraftsman Thomas Frank Spiby

The Second World War
Peatling Parva's war dead

Phillip Hunt
Rank: Aircraftsman 1st Class
Number: 1430083
Regiment, Corps etc:
290 Squadron, Royal Air Force (Volunteer Reserve)
Military Service: After his training, Phillip Hunt was posted to 290 Squadron, which was formed in 1943 to provide training for anti-aircraft units. The aeroplanes of the squadron were employed in towing targets for the anti-aircraft batteries.
Date and circumstances of Death: Phillip Hunt was killed in a 'plane crash in Scotland.
Age: 21
Buried: Bruntingthorpe churchyard
Family: Phillip was the youngest of the fourteen children of John Hunt and his wife, Mary Elizabeth Ann Lord, who had married on 16 March 1899. Their children were Susan, Florence, Rose, Frances, William, Frank William (baptised 1911) George Arthur (1914) Thomas, Joseph, and Marjorie Joan (all baptised in 1916) Frederick Victor and Walter Ernest (1919) Harold Martin (1920) and Phillip (1923).

Cameron Lawrie
Rank: Steward
Number: D/LX24537
Regiment, Corps etc:
Royal Navy (HMS *Dorsetshire*)
Date and circumstances of Death: Cameron Lawrie was killed when his ship, the 13,000 ton cruiser, *Dorsetshire*, was sunk by Japanese carrier-borne aircraft west of Ceylon on 5th April 1942.
Age: 19
Buried: Cameron Lawrie is remembered on the war memorial at Plymouth.
Family: Cameron was the son of William and Nancy Lawrie, of Saltcoats, Ayrshire.
Notes: Cameron was employed as a footman by Mrs Gemmell, of Peatling Parva Hall. The Gemmells were themselves Scottish and a number of their employees at the Hall were also from Scotland.

Sidney George Turner

Rank: Leading Stoker
Number: C/KX 583048
Regiment, Corps etc:
Royal Navy (HMS *Hurst Castle*)
Date and circumstances of Death:
HMS *Hurst Castle*, a Castle-class corvette, was serving as an escort to convoy CU-36, when torpedoed by U482 at 8.22 a.m. on 1st September 1944. Leading stoker Turner was not amongst the survivors brought ashore by HMS *Ambuscade*.
Age: 30
Buried: Sidney Turner is remembered on the Chatham Naval Memorial.
Family: Sidney was the son of James Clarke Turner and his wife, Alice Mabel Prentice. Sidney was born on 14 May 1917. He had two brothers; James Douglas Joseph (born 1916) and Desmond Henry (1923) and one sister, Brenda Olive (born 1920).

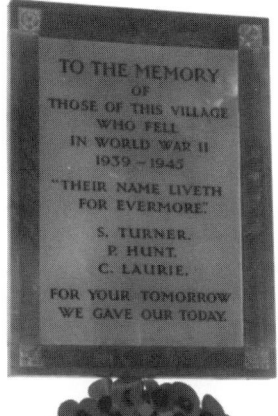

*War Memorial 1939-45
St Andrews Church, Peatling Parva*

THE SECOND WORLD WAR
SHEARSBY'S WAR DEAD

Maurice Arthur Garner

Rank: Private
Number: 4860094
Regiment, Corps etc:
1st Battalion,
Leicestershire Regiment
Date and circumstances of Death:
22nd December 1941
Age: 22
Buried: Taiping War Cemetery, Malaysia; joint grave 2. H. 2-3 He is also remembered on his parents' gravestone in Shearsby churchyard.
Family: Maurice was the son of Ernest and Evelyn Garner.

Short history of the Leicestershire Regiment

1688 - 1881

On September 27th 1688 a commission was issued to Colonel Solomon Richards to raise a regiment of foot. From 1688 to 1751 the regiment was known by the name of its various colonels. The regiment saw service in the Flanders from 1694 to 1697, before moving to Ireland. In 1701 the regiment moved to the continent of Europe, and took part in the War of the Spanish Succession. In 1709 the unit returned to England, moving to Minorca in 1725.

In 1751 a royal warrant assigned numbers to the regiments of the line, and the unit became the 17th Regiment of Foot. The 17th were in service during the American War of Independence, landing in Boston on New Year's Day 1776. The regiment's performance at the Battle of Princetown was commemorated in the addition of an unbroken laurel wreath to its insignia. The regiment moved to Nova Scotia before returning to England in 1786.

A royal warrant dated August 31, 1782 bestowed county titles on all regiments of foot that did not already have a special designation "to cultivate a connection with the County which might at all times be useful towards recruiting".

The regiment became the 17th (Leicestershire) Regiment of Foot. The regiment was increased to two battalions in 1799 and both battalions served in the Netherlands before the second was disbanded in 1802. In 1804 the 17th moved to India, and remained there until 1823. In 1825 the regiment was granted the badge of a "royal tiger" to recall their long service in the sub-continent.

The regiment returned to India in 1837, and then took part in the First Afghan War from 1838 to 1842. The 17th next came under fire in the Crimean War from 1854 to 1856.

In 1858 a second battalion was raised. The battalions served in Afghanistan, Burma, Canada.

1881 - 1914

The Childers reforms of 1881 created multi-battalion regiments. Each regiment had a designated regimental district and also incorporated the local militia and rifle volunteers. Regiments of foot were no longer to have numbers, but were to bear a territorial title. The Leicestershire Regiment was accordingly formed on July 1, 1881. The regimental depot was at Glen Parva, and the regiment consisted of:

* The 1st and 2nd Battalions (formerly the 1st and 2nd battalions of the 17th Foot)
* 3rd (Militia) Battalion (formerly the Leicestershire Militia)
* 1st Leicestershire Rifle Volunteer Corps, redesignated as the 1st Volunteer Battalion in 1883

The 1st and 3rd battalions fought in the Second Boer War 1899 - 1902. In 1908, with the creation of the Territorial Force, the 1st Volunteer Battalion formed the 4th and 5th Battalions (TF). There was a minor controversy in the same year, when new colours were issued to the 1st Battalion to replace those of the 17th foot. A green tiger had been shown on the old colours and the regiment refused to take the new issue into use. The issue was resolved when the regiment received permission for the royal tiger emblazoned on the regimental colours to be coloured green with gold stripes.

1914 - 1918

In the First World War, the regiment increased from five to nineteen battalions which served in France and Flanders, Mesopotamia and Palestine. The regiment lost approximately 6,000 dead in the four years of war.

1918 - 1939

The regiment reverted to its pre-war establishment in 1919. The 1st Battalion was involved in the Irish War of Independence 1920 - 1922, before moving to various overseas garrisons including Cyprus, Egypt and India. The 2nd Battalion was in India, Sudan, Germany and Palestine.

The 3rd (Militia) Battalion was placed in "suspended animation" in 1921, eventually being formally disbanded in 1953. In 1936 the 4th Battalion was converted to an anti-aircraft unit of the Royal Engineers, later part of the Royal Artillery. The size of the Territorial Army was doubled in 1939, and consequently the 1/5th and 2/5th Battalions were formed from the existing 5th.

1939 - 1945

Battalions of the regiment served in many theatres of the war, including Burma, Greece, Italy, North Africa, North West Europe and Norway.

1945 - 1964

In 1946 the regiment was granted "royal" status, becoming the Royal Leicestershire Regiment. In 1948, in common with all other infantry regiments, the 2nd Battalion was abolished. The 5th Battalion (TA) had been reformed in 1947.

In 1948 the regiment became part of the Forester Brigade, sharing a depot at Warwick with The Royal Warwickshire Regiment, The Royal Lincolnshire Regiment

and The Sherwood Foresters. Glen Parva was downgraded to regimental headquarters.
The 1st Battalion served in the Korean War from 1951 to 1952. They subsequently moved to England (exercising the freedom of the City of Leicester in 1952), Germany, Suden, Cyprus, Brunei and Aden.
In 1961 the territorial 5th Battalion absorbed the anti-aircraft successor to the former 4th Battalion to become the 4th/5th Battalion.
In 1963 the Forester Brigade was dissolved, with the Royal Leicesters and Royal Lincolns moving to the East Anglian Brigade where they joined the the 1st, 2nd and 3rd East Anglian Regiments.

Abolition

On September 1st 1964 the regiments of the East Anglian Brigade became The Royal Anglian Regiment. The 1st Battalion, Royal Leicestershire Regiment became the 4th (Leicestershire) Battalion, The Royal Anglian Regiment. The "Leicestershire" subtitle was removed on July 1st 1968 and the battalion was disbanded in 1975. The Royal Leicestershire heritage was included in the new regiment's button design, which features the royal tiger within an unbroken wreath.

The 4th/5th Battalion, Royal Leicestershire Regiment continued to exist as a territorial unit of the Royal Anglians until its disbandment in 1967.

Regimental history taken from Wikipedia based on information from 'The Tigers - a short history of the Royal Leicestershire Regiment' by J.M.K. Spurling (1969). Military History Society Bulletin, Special Issue No.1, 1968. 'The Royal Leicestershire Regiment' by T.F. Mills.

Acknowledgments

Pam Sansome	Lutterworth
Ellen Warner	Countesthorpe
Ann Swatland	Countesthorpe
Alan Peet	Aylestone
John Taylor	Aylestone
Wendy Laxton	Countesthorpe
Malcomb Glass	Wigston Magna
Robert N. Harrison	Lymington, Hants.
Derick Seaton	Leicester
David & Glory Burley	Countesthorpe
Ruth Findley	Countesthorpe
John Morris	Crowland, Lincs.
Gerald King	Narborough
Roger Johnson	Countesthorpe
Angela Skerrett	Countesthorpe
Douglas Elliott	Leicester
Alfred Oldershaw	Countesthorpe
Eva Morris	Countesthorpe
Freda Dixon	Burbage
Judith Evans	Brighton
Stella Hubbard [Deceased]	Countesthorpe
David & Jill Thornton	Saddington
Brenda Russell	Kettering
Kathleen Lord	Countesthorpe
Eileen Cosby	Countesthorpe
Dr Mike & Jane Thompson	Countesthorpe
Josephine Howes	Fakenham
Evelyn Burn	Glen Parva
Valerie Hunt	Countesthorpe
Arnold Smith	Countesthorpe
Connie Ball	Whetstone
Murial Harfield	Newbold Verdon
D.R. Mawby	Arnesby
Shirley Hensman	Wigston Magna
Margaret Godsmark	Shearsby
John & Nora Burton	Shearsby
Kathleen Sheffield	Countesthorpe
E. Garrett	Countesthorpe
Greg Chapman	Markfield
Patrick Hunt	Countesthorpe
Diane Lee	Countesthorpe
Elaine Edwards	Countesthorpe
Joan Richardson & Daughter Patricia	

Special thanks to **Robin Jenkins** and the staff of the Record Office for Rutland, Leicester and Leicestershire at Long Street, Wigston Magna.

The Stuart Cosby Memorial Trust

The Countesthorpe and Foston Heritage Group

The Countesthorpe Herald
for a grant towards research costs.

Eileen Bates for her computer skills and my good friend **Margaret Mitton** for the use of her car and time when taking me to call on people out of the village and **Pam Ward** for her encouragement.